ASK ME

T0055533

11 December 1974
At Sisters — the whole roof is up, the house enclosed.

Here, touched with genius, the girl
turned aside: every value has
commitment for its foundation—
what if you questioned? Held the value
but questioned? She became Miss
America, though no one knew.
Outside of America her symptoms
became footnotes in annals of the learned.

Sometime when the river is ice, ask me
mistakes I have made, ask me whether what I have
done is my life. Others have come
in their slow way into my thoughts, and
some have tried to help or to hurt.
Ask me what difference their strongest
hate or love has made.

You and I can then turn
and look at the silent river and wait.
We will know the current is there,
hidden, and there are comings and goings
miles away that hold the stillness
exactly before us. If the river says anything,
whatever it says is my answer.
What the river says

First draft of "Ask Me," December 11, 1974 (reduced).
From the William Stafford Archives.

Also by William Stafford

POETRY

Another World Instead: The Early Poems of William Stafford 1937–1947
The Way It Is: New and Selected Poems
Even in Quiet Places
My Name Is William Tell
Passwords
An Oregon Message
Smoke's Way
A Glass Face in the Rain
Stories That Could Be True
Someday, Maybe
Allegiances
The Rescued Year
Traveling through the Dark
West of Your City

PROSE

Every War Has Two Losers: William Stafford on Peace and War
Crossing Unmarked Snow: Further Views on the Writer's Vocation
The Answers Are inside the Mountains: Meditations on the Writing Life
You Must Revise Your Life
Writing the Australian Crawl: Views on the Writer's Vocation
Down in My Heart: Peace Witness in War Time

ASK ME

100 Essential Poems

WILLIAM STAFFORD

Edited by Kim Stafford

Graywolf Press

Poems included in this volume were previously published in *The Way It Is: New and Selected Poems* (Graywolf Press, 1998) and *Another World Instead: The Early Poems of William Stafford 1937–1947* (Graywolf Press, 2008).

This publication is made possible, in part, by the voters of Minnesota through a Minnesota State Arts Board Operating Support grant, thanks to a legislative appropriation from the arts and cultural heritage fund, and through grants from the National Endowment for the Arts and the Wells Fargo Foundation Minnesota. Significant support has also been provided by Target, the McKnight Foundation, Amazon.com, and other generous contributions from foundations, corporations, and individuals. To these organizations and individuals we offer our heartfelt thanks.

Published by Graywolf Press
250 Third Avenue North, Suite 600
Minneapolis, Minnesota 55401

www.graywolfpress.org

Published in the United States of America

ISBN 978-1-55597-664-4

4 6 8 9 7 5

Library of Congress Control Number: 2013946920

Cover design: Jeenee Lee Design

Cover photo: Robert B. Miller

Contents

Preface

William Stafford was born in 1914, the first year of the Great War. As a child, he heard drums in the military parade. At the edge of town, he watched the Klan march. He chopped weeds in the sugar beet field. He worked in an oil refinery. His paper route sustained the family for a time. And when he started writing during World War II, in a camp for conscientious objectors, he wrote about trees, and evening, and quiet at the margins. He wrote about the citizens of Dresden. He was spared the need to hate. Something deeper was at stake.

A hungry reader of philosophy, his lifelong companions were Nietzsche, Kierkegaard, Pascal, and Wittgenstein. But so were the thousands who sent him their poems, and received an immediate reply. "Let's talk recklessly," he would say. He wrote rituals, notes, lists, gestures, letters, poems—and invited others into those spaces. "I must be willingly fallible," he wrote, "to deserve a place in the realm where miracles happen."

At a reading, he would hold up his left hand, starting into a poem: "This is the hand I dipped in the Missouri. . . ." Or if he found himself in another country, he would name the local river. In the poem that gives this book its title, he wrote, "What the river says, that is what I say." He read these poems in Iran under the Shah, in Poland, Egypt, Pakistan, India, Nepal.

With his habit of writing every day before dawn, he composed twenty thousand poems. Of these, four thousand were published in magazines. He had a cardboard box in his office labeled "Abandoned Poems." When I reached in a few days after my father died to take one at random, it was startling, imperfect, exploratory. I remembered his claim, "I would trade everything I have ever written for the next thing."

He traveled for poetry—sometimes thirty readings in thirty days. He was an ambassador for the possibility of peace through poetry. The calendar was black with engagements. At a reading, following one of his deft, quiet offerings, a listener helplessly spoke aloud, "I could have written that." And William Stafford, looking kindly at the speaker, replied, "But you didn't." A beat of silence. "But you could write your own."

You could write your own. What a democratic idea. Each of us could write our own poem, our own proposal for peace, our own aphoristic meditation at the un-national monument, our own consolation, manifesto, blessing. "The field of writing will never be crowded," he told me once, "not because people can't write, but they don't think they can." His life as teacher and witness and corresponding friend advocated the pen in hand, the moving pen, "your own way of looking at things."

A hundred years after his birth, from the fifty books he published in his lifetime and the dozen published since, *Ask Me* offers these one hundred essential poems of William Stafford, from the indelible scene described in "Traveling through the Dark" to the challenging questions presented in "You Reading This, Be Ready."

This book will help us all be ready. "The greatest ownership of all," he said, "is to look around and understand." For us, poem by poem, he looked at the world—and the world was mysterious, dark, enticing.

Kim Stafford

ASK ME

A Story That Could Be True

If you were exchanged in the cradle and
your real mother died
without ever telling the story
then no one knows your name,
and somewhere in the world
your father is lost and needs you
but you are far away.

He can never find
how true you are, how ready.
When the great wind comes
and the robberies of the rain
you stand on the corner shivering.
The people who go by—
you wonder at their calm.

They miss the whisper that runs
any day in your mind,
"Who are you really, wanderer?"—
and the answer you have to give
no matter how dark and cold
the world around you is:
"Maybe I'm a king."

Fifteen

South of the bridge on Seventeenth
I found back of the willows one summer
day a motorcycle with engine running
as it lay on its side, ticking over
slowly in the high grass. I was fifteen.

I admired all that pulsing gleam, the
shiny flanks, the demure headlights
fringed where it lay; I led it gently
to the road and stood with that
companion, ready and friendly. I was fifteen.

We could find the end of a road, meet
the sky on out Seventeenth. I thought about
hills, and patting the handle got back a
confident opinion. On the bridge we indulged
a forward feeling, a tremble. I was fifteen.

Thinking, back farther in the grass I found
the owner, just coming to, where he had flipped
over the rail. He had blood on his hand, was pale—
I helped him walk to his machine. He ran his hand
over it, called me good man, roared away.

I stood there, fifteen.

Vocation

This dream the world is having about itself
includes a trace on the plains of the Oregon trail,
a groove in the grass my father showed us all
one day while meadowlarks were trying to tell
something better about to happen.

I dreamed the trace to the mountains, over the hills,
and there a girl who belonged wherever she was.
But then my mother called us back to the car:
she was afraid; she always blamed the place,
the time, anything my father planned.

Now both of my parents, the long line through the plain,
the meadowlarks, the sky, the world's whole dream
remain, and I hear him say while I stand between the two,
helpless, both of them part of me:
"Your job is to find what the world is trying to be."

Ask Me

Some time when the river is ice ask me
mistakes I have made. Ask me whether
what I have done is my life. Others
have come in their slow way into
my thought, and some have tried to help
or to hurt: ask me what difference
their strongest love or hate has made.

I will listen to what you say.
You and I can turn and look
at the silent river and wait. We know
the current is there, hidden; and there
are comings and goings from miles away
that hold the stillness exactly before us.
What the river says, that is what I say.

The Way It Is

There's a thread you follow. It goes among
things that change. But it doesn't change.
People wonder about what you are pursuing.
You have to explain about the thread.
But it is hard for others to see.
While you hold it you can't get lost.
Tragedies happen; people get hurt
or die; and you suffer and get old.
Nothing you do can stop time's unfolding.
You don't ever let go of the thread.

A Message from the Wanderer

Today outside your prison I stand
and rattle my walking stick: Prisoners, listen;
you have relatives outside. And there are
thousands of ways to escape.

Years ago I bent my skill to keep my
cell locked, had chains smuggled to me in pies,
and shouted my plans to jailers;
but always new plans occurred to me,
or the new heavy locks bent hinges off,
or some stupid jailer would forget
and leave the keys.

Inside, I dreamed of constellations—
those feeding creatures outlined by stars,
their skeletons a darkness between jewels,
heroes that exist only where they are not.

Thus freedom always came nibbling my thought,
just as—often, in light, on the open hills—
you can pass an antelope and not know
and look back, and then—even before you see—
there is something wrong about the grass.
And then you see.

That's the way everything in the world is waiting.

Now—these few more words, and then I'm
gone: Tell everyone just to remember
their names, and remind others, later, when we
find each other. Tell the little ones
to cry and then go to sleep, curled up
where they can. And if any of us get lost,
if any of us cannot come all the way—
remember: there will come a time when
all we have said and all we have hoped
will be all right.

There will be that form in the grass.

Traveling through the Dark

Traveling through the dark I found a deer
dead on the edge of the Wilson River road.
It is usually best to roll them into the canyon:
that road is narrow; to swerve might make more dead.

By glow of the tail-light I stumbled back of the car
and stood by the heap, a doe, a recent killing;
she had stiffened already, almost cold.
I dragged her off; she was large in the belly.

My fingers touching her side brought me the reason—
her side was warm; her fawn lay there waiting,
alive, still, never to be born.
Beside that mountain road I hesitated.

The car aimed ahead its lowered parking lights;
under the hood purred the steady engine.
I stood in the glare of the warm exhaust turning red;
around our group I could hear the wilderness listen.

I thought hard for us all—my only swerving—,
then pushed her over the edge into the river.

Mein Kampf

In those reaches of the night when your thoughts
burrow in, or at some stabbed interval
pinned by a recollection in daylight,
a better self begs its hands out to you:

That bitter tracery your life wove
looms forth, and the jagged times haggle
and excruciate your reaching palms again—
"A dull knife hurts most."

Old mistakes come calling: no life
happens just once. Whatever snags
even the edge of your days will abide.
You are a turtle with all the years on your back.

Your head sinks down into the mud.
You must bear it. You need a thick shell in that rain.

You Reading This, Be Ready

Starting here, what do you want to remember?
How sunlight creeps along a shining floor?
What scent of old wood hovers, what softened
sound from outside fills the air?

Will you ever bring a better gift for the world
than the breathing respect that you carry
wherever you go right now? Are you waiting
for time to show you some better thoughts?

When you turn around, starting here, lift this
new glimpse that you found; carry into evening
all that you want from this day. This interval you spent
reading or hearing this, keep it for life—

What can anyone give you greater than now,
starting here, right in this room, when you turn around?

Security

Tomorrow will have an island. Before night
I always find it. Then on to the next island.
These places hidden in the day separate
and come forward if you beckon.
But you have to know they are there before they exist.

Some time there will be a tomorrow without any island.
So far, I haven't let that happen, but after
I'm gone others may become faithless and careless.
Before them will tumble the wide unbroken sea,
and without any hope they will stare at the horizon.

So to you, Friend, I confide my secret:
to be a discoverer you hold close whatever
you find, and after a while you decide
what it is. Then, secure in where you have been,
you turn to the open sea and let go.

Thinking for Berky

In the late night listening from bed
I have joined the ambulance or the patrol
screaming toward some drama, the kind of end
that Berky must have some day, if she isn't dead.

The wildest of all, her father and mother cruel,
farming out there beyond the old stone quarry
where highschool lovers parked their lurching cars,
Berky learned to love in that dark school.

Early her face was turned away from home
toward any hardworking place; but still her soul,
with terrible things to do, was alive, looking out
for the rescue that—surely, some day—would have to come.

Windiest nights, Berky, I have thought for you,
and no matter how lucky I've been I've touched wood.
There are things not solved in our town though tomorrow came:
there are things time passing can never make come true.

We live in an occupied country, misunderstood;
justice will take us millions of intricate moves.
Sirens will hunt down Berky, you survivors in your beds
listening through the night, so far and good.

Why I Am Happy

Now has come, an easy time. I let it
roll. There is a lake somewhere
so blue and far nobody owns it.
A wind comes by and a willow listens
gracefully.

I hear all this, every summer. I laugh
and cry for every turn of the world,
its terribly cold, innocent spin.
That lake stays blue and free; it goes
on and on.

And I know where it is.

A Ritual to Read to Each Other

If you don't know the kind of person I am
and I don't know the kind of person you are
a pattern that others made may prevail in the world
and following the wrong god home we may miss our star.

For there is many a small betrayal in the mind,
a shrug that lets the fragile sequence break
sending with shouts the horrible errors of childhood
storming out to play through the broken dyke.

And as elephants parade holding each elephant's tail,
but if one wanders the circus won't find the park,
I call it cruel and maybe the root of all cruelty
to know what occurs but not recognize the fact.

And so I appeal to a voice, to something shadowy,
a remote important region in all who talk:
though we could fool each other, we should consider—
lest the parade of our mutual life get lost in the dark.

For it is important that awake people be awake,
or a breaking line may discourage them back to sleep;
the signals we give—yes or no, or maybe—
should be clear: the darkness around us is deep.

Serving with Gideon

Now I remember: in our town the druggist
prescribed Coca-Cola mostly, in tapered
glasses to us, and to the elevator
man in a paper cup, so he could
drink it elsewhere because he was black.

And now I remember The Legion—gambling
in the back room, and no women but girls, old boys
who ran the town. They were generous,
to their sons or the sons of friends.
And of course I was almost one.

I remember winter light closing
its great blue fist slowly eastward
along the street, and the dark then, deep
as war, arched over a radio show
called the thirties in the great old U.S.A.

Look down, stars—I was almost
one of the boys. My mother was folding
her handkerchief; the library seethed and sparked;
right and wrong arced; and carefully
I walked with my cup toward the elevator man.

Easter Morning

Maybe someone comes to the door and says,
"Repent," and you say, "Come on in," and it's
Jesus. That's when all you ever did, or said,
or even thought, suddenly wakes up again and
sings out, "I'm still here," and you know it's true.
You just shiver alive and are left standing
there suddenly brought to account: saved.

Except, maybe that someone says, "I've got a deal
for you." And you listen, because that's how
you're trained—they told you, "Always hear both sides."
So then the slick voice can sell you anything, even
Hell, which is what you're getting by listening.
Well, what should you do? I'd say always go to
the door, yes, but keep the screen locked. Then,
while you hold the Bible in one hand, lean forward
and say carefully, "Jesus?"

Assurance

You will never be alone, you hear so deep
a sound when autumn comes. Yellow
pulls across the hills and thrums,
or the silence after lightning before it says
its names—and then the clouds' wide-mouthed
apologies. You were aimed from birth:
you will never be alone. Rain
will come, a gutter filled, an Amazon,
long aisles—you never heard so deep a sound,
moss on rock, and years. You turn your head—
that's what the silence meant: *you're not alone.*
The whole wide world pours down.

Our Story

Remind me again—together we
trace our strange journey, find
each other, come on laughing.
Some time we'll cross where life
ends. We'll both look back
as far as forever, that first day.
I'll touch you—a new world then.
Stars will move a different way.
We'll both end. We'll both begin.

Remind me again.

The Little Ways That Encourage Good Fortune

Wisdom is having things right in your life
and knowing why.
If you do not have things right in your life
you will be overwhelmed:
you may be heroic, but you will not be wise.
If you have things right in your life
but do not know why,
you are just lucky, and you will not move
in the little ways that encourage good fortune.

The saddest are those not right in their lives
who are acting to make things right for others:
they act only from the self—
and that self will never be right:
no luck, no help, no wisdom.

A Gesture toward an Unfound Renaissance

There was the slow girl in art class,
less able to say where our lessons led: we
learned so fast she could not follow us.
But at the door each day I looked back
at her rich distress, knowing almost enough
to find a better art inside the lesson.

And then, late at night, when the whole town
was alone, the current below the rumbly bridge
at Main Street would go an extra swirl
and gurgle, once, by the pilings;
and at my desk at home, or when our house
opened above my bed toward the stars,
I would hear that one intended lonely sound,
the signature of the day, the ratchet of time
taking me a step toward here, now, and this
look back through the door that always closes.

Saint Matthew and All

Lorene—we thought she'd come home. But
it got late, and then days. Now
it has been years. Why shouldn't she,
if she wanted? I would: something comes
along, a sunny day, you start walking;
you meet a person who says, "Follow me,"
and things lead on.

Usually, it wouldn't happen, but sometimes
the neighbors notice your car is gone, the
patch of oil in the driveway, and it fades.
They forget.

In the Bible it happened—fishermen, Levites.
They just went away and kept going. Thomas,
away off in India, never came back.

But Lorene—it was a stranger maybe, and he
said, "Your life, I need it." And nobody else did.

A Dedication

We stood by the library. It was an August night.
Priests and sisters of hundreds of unsaid creeds
passed us going their separate pondered roads.
We watched them cross under the corner light.

Freights on the edge of town were carrying away
flatcars of steel to be made into secret guns;
we knew, being human, that they were enemy guns,
and we were somehow vowed to poverty.

No one stopped or looked long or held out a hand.
They were following orders received from hour to hour,
so many signals, all strange, from a foreign power:
But tomorrow, you whispered, *peace may flow over the land.*

At that corner in a flash of lightning we two stood;
that glimpse we had will stare through the dark forever:
on the poorest roads we would be walkers and beggars,
toward some deathless meeting involving a crust of bread.

Learning

A piccolo played, then a drum.
Feet began to come—a part
of the music. Here came a horse,
clippety clop, away.

My mother said, "Don't run—
the army is after someone
other than us. If you stay
you'll learn our enemy."

Then he came, the speaker. He stood
in the square. He told us who
to hate. I watched my mother's face,
its quiet. "That's him," she said.

Objector

In line at lunch I cross my fork and spoon
to ward off complicity—the ordered life
our leaders have offered us. Thin as a knife,
our chance to live depends on such a sign
while others talk and The Pentagon from the moon
is bouncing exact commands: "Forget your faith;
be ready for whatever it takes to win: we face
annihilation unless all citizens get in line."

I bow and cross my fork and spoon: somewhere
other citizens more fearfully bow
in a place terrorized by their kind of oppressive state.
Our signs both mean, "You hostages over there
will never be slaughtered by my act." Our vows
cross: never to kill and call it fate.

At the Un-National Monument along the Canadian Border

This is the field where the battle did not happen,
where the unknown soldier did not die.
This is the field where grass joined hands,
where no monument stands,
and the only heroic thing is the sky.

Birds fly here without any sound,
unfolding their wings across the open.
No people killed—or were killed—on this ground
hallowed by neglect and an air so tame
that people celebrate it by forgetting its name.

For the Unknown Enemy

This monument is for the unknown
good in our enemies. Like a picture
their life began to appear: they
gathered at home in the evening
and sang. Above their fields they saw
a new sky. A holiday came
and they carried the baby to the park
for a party. Sunlight surrounded them.

Here we glimpse what our minds long turned
away from. The great mutual
blindness darkened that sunlight in the park,
and the sky that was new, and the holidays.
This monument says that one afternoon
we stood here letting a part of our minds
escape. They came back, but different.
Enemy: one day we glimpsed your life.

This monument is for you.

At the Bomb Testing Site

At noon in the desert a panting lizard
waited for history, its elbows tense,
watching the curve of a particular road
as if something might happen.

It was looking at something farther off
than people could see, an important scene
acted in stone for little selves
at the flute end of consequences.

There was just a continent without much on it
under a sky that never cared less.
Ready for a change, the elbows waited.
The hands gripped hard on the desert.

These Mornings

Watch our smoke curdle up out of the chimney
    into the canyon channel of air.
The wind shakes it free over the trees
    and hurries it into nothing.

Today there is more smoke in the world
    than ever before.
There are more cities going into the sky,
    helplessly, than ever before.

The cities today are going away into the sky,
    and what is left is going into the earth.

This is what happens when a city is bombed:
    Part of that city goes away into the sky,
    And part of that city goes into the earth.
And that is what happens to the people when a city is bombed:
    Part of them goes away into the sky,
    And part of them goes into the earth.
And what is left, for us, between the sky and the earth
    is a scar.

Distractions

Think about Gypsies—
like smoke in the evening they cross a border.
They don't believe in it, and they say if God
doesn't care nobody cares. In the morning
their wagons are gone, carrying their stories
away. They like the sound of a wheel
and have given up owning a place. They roll
beyond old newspapers and broken glass and
start a new campfire. Sometimes, going up
a steep hill, they get off and walk forward
and whisper the oldest secret in the world
into the ears of their horses.

Watching the Jet Planes Dive

We must go back and find a trail on the ground
back of the forest and mountain on the slow land;
we must begin to circle on the intricate sod.
By such wild beginnings without help we may find
the small trail on through the buffalo-bean vines.

We must go back with noses and the palms of our hands,
and climb over the map in far places, everywhere,
and lie down whenever there is doubt and sleep there.
If roads are unconnected we must make a path,
no matter how far it is, or how lowly we arrive.

We must find something forgotten by everyone alive,
and make some fabulous gesture when the sun goes down
as they do by custom in little Mexico towns
where they crawl for some ritual up a rocky steep.
The jet planes dive; we must travel on our knees.

Poetry

Its door opens near. It's a shrine
by the road, it's a flower in the parking lot
of The Pentagon, it says, "Look around,
listen. Feel the air." It interrupts
international telephone lines with a tune.
When traffic lines jam, it gets out
and dances on the bridge. If great people
get distracted by fame they forget
this essential kind of breathing
and they die inside their gold shell.
When caravans cross deserts
it is the secret treasure hidden under the jewels.

Sometimes commanders take us over, and they
try to impose their whole universe,
how to succeed by daily calculation:
I can't eat that bread.

The Star in the Hills

A star hit in the hills behind our house
up where the grass turns brown touching the sky.

Meteors have hit the world before, but this was near,
and since TV; few saw, but many felt the shock.
The state of California owns that land
(and out from shore three miles), and any stars
that come will be roped off and viewed on week days 8 to 5.

A guard who took the oath of loyalty and denied
any police record told me this:
"If you don't have a police record yet
you could take the oath and get a job
if California should be hit by another star."

"I'd promise to be loyal to California
and to guard any stars that hit it," I said,
"or any place three miles out from shore,
unless the star was bigger than the state—
in which case, I'd be loyal to *it*."

But he said no exceptions were allowed,
and he leaned against the state-owned meteor
so calm and puffed a cork-tip cigarette
that I looked down and traced with my foot in the dust
and thought again and said, "OK—any star."

Peace Walk

We wondered what our walk should mean,
taking that un-march quietly;
the sun stared at our signs—"Thou shalt not kill."

Men by a tavern said, "Those foreigners . . ."
to a woman with a fur, who turned away—
like an elevator going down, their look at us.

Along a curb, their signs lined across,
a picket line stopped and stared
the whole width of the street, at ours: "Unfair."

Above our heads the sound truck blared—
by the park, under the autumn trees—
it said that love could fill the atmosphere:

Occur, slow the other fallout, unseen,
on islands everywhere—fallout, falling
unheard. We held our poster up to shade our eyes.

At the end we just walked away;
no one was there to tell us where to leave the signs.

Explaining the Big One

Remember that leader with the funny mustache?—
liked flags and marching?—gave loyalty
a bad name? Didn't drink, they say,
but liked music, and was jolly, sometimes.

And then the one with the big mustache
and the wrinkled uniform, always jovial
for the camera but eliminated malcontents
by the millions. He was our friend, I think.

Women? Oh yes, women. They danced
and sang for the soldiers or volunteered
their help. We loved them, except Tokyo
Rose—didn't we kill her, afterward?

Our own leaders?—the jaunty cigarette holder,
the one with the cigar. . . . Remember the pearl-handled
revolvers? And Ike, who played golf. It was us
against the bad guys, then. You should have been there.

Entering History

Remember the line in the sand?
You were there, on the telly, part of
the military. You didn't want to
give it but they took your money
for those lethal tanks and the bombs.

Minorities, they don't have a country
even if they vote: "Thanks, anyway,"
the majority says, and you are left there
staring at the sand and the line they drew,
calling it a challenge, calling it "ours."

Where was your money when the tanks
grumbled past? Which bombs did you buy
for the death rain that fell? Which year's
taxes put that fire to the town
where the screaming began?

"Shall we have that singing . . ."

Shall we have that singing in the evening?
For between the stars and our star there is no one.
And we must sleep again.
We rest the hands, not dangerous, on the wool.
And we place pillows under the turning head.

Quietly now, no moving,
Was there something forgotten?

(The losing one neglects and calls it winning.)
Help each other.
Have that singing in the evening.

In the Night Desert

The Apache word for love twists
    then numbs the tongue:
Uttered once clear, said—
    never that word again.

"Cousin," you call, or "Sister" and one
    more word that spins
In the dust: a talk-flake
    chipped like obsidian.

The girl who hears this flake and
    follows you into the dark
Turns at a touch: the night desert
    forever behind her back.

The Concealment: Ishi, the Last Wild Indian

A rock, a leaf, mud, even the grass
Ishi the shadow man had to put back where it was.
In order to live he had to hide that he did.
His deep canyon he kept unmarked for the world,
and only his face became lined, because no one saw it
and it therefore didn't make any difference.

If he appeared, he died; and he was the last. Erased
footprints, berries that purify the breath, rituals
before dawn with water—even the dogs roamed a land
unspoiled by Ishi who used to own it, with his aunt
and uncle, whose old limbs bound in willow bark finally
stopped and were hidden under the rocks, in sweet leaves.

We ought to help change that kind of premature suicide,
the existence gradually mottled away till the heartbeat
blends and the messages all go one way from the world
and disappear inward: Ishi lived. It was all right
for him to make a track. In California now where his opposites
unmistakably dwell we wander their streets

And sometimes whisper his name—
"Ishi."

Bess

Ours are the streets where Bess first met her
cancer. She went to work every day past the
secure houses. At her job in the library
she arranged better and better flowers, and when
students asked for books her hand went out
to help. In the last year of her life
she had to keep her friends from knowing
how happy they were. She listened while they
complained about food or work or the weather.
And the great national events danced
their grotesque, fake importance. Always

Pain moved where she moved. She walked
ahead; it came. She hid; it found her.
No one ever served another so truly;
no enemy ever meant so strong a hate.
It was almost as if there was no room
left for her on earth. But she remembered
where joy used to live. She straightened its flowers;
she did not weep when she passed its houses;
and when finally she pulled into a tiny corner
and slipped from pain, her hand opened
again, and the streets opened, and she wished all well.

American Gothic

If we see better through tiny,
grim glasses, we like to wear
tiny, grim glasses.
Our parents willed us this
view. It's tundra? We love it.

We travel our kind of
Renaissance: barnfuls of hay,
whole voyages of corn, and
a book that flickers its
halo in the parlor.

Poverty plus confidence equals
pioneers. We never doubted.

Report to Crazy Horse

All the Sioux were defeated. Our clan
got poor, but a few got richer.
They fought two wars. I did not
take part. No one remembers your vision
or even your real name. Now
the children go to town and like
loud music. I married a Christian.

Crazy Horse, it is not fair
to hide a new vision from you.
In our schools we are learning
to take aim when we talk, and we have
found out our enemies. They shift when
words do; they even change and hide
in every person. A teacher here says
hurt or scorned people are places
where real enemies hide. He says
we should not hurt or scorn anyone,
but help them. And I will tell you
in a brave way, the way Crazy Horse
talked: that teacher is right.

I will tell you a strange thing:
at the rodeo, close to the grandstand,
I saw a farm lady scared by a blown
piece of paper; and at that place
horses and policemen were no longer
frightening, but suffering faces were,
and the hunched-over backs of the old.

Crazy Horse, tell me if I am right:
these are the things we thought we were
doing something about.

In your life you saw many strange things,
and I will tell you another: now I salute
the white man's flag. But when I salute
I hold my hand alertly on the heartbeat
and remember all of us and how we depend
on a steady pulse together. There are those
who salute because they fear other flags
or mean to use ours to chase them:
I must not allow my part of saluting
to mean this. All of our promises,
our generous sayings to each other, our
honorable intentions—those I affirm
when I salute. At these times it is like
shutting my eyes and joining a religious
colony at prayer in the gray dawn
in the deep aisles of a church.

Now I have told you about new times.
Yes, I know others will report
different things. They have been caught
by weak ways. I tell you straight
the way it is now, and it is our way,
the way we were trying to find.

The chokecherries along our valley
still bear a bright fruit. There is good
pottery clay north of here. I remember
our old places. When I pass the Musselshell
I run my hand along those old grooves in the rock.

For My Young Friends Who Are Afraid

There is a country to cross you will
find in the corner of your eye, in
the quick slip of your foot—air far
down, a snap that might have caught.
And maybe for you, for me, a high, passing
voice that finds its way by being
afraid. That country is there, for us,
carried as it is crossed. What you fear
will not go away: it will take you into
yourself and bless you and keep you.
That's the world, and we all live there.

Listening

My father could hear a little animal step,
or a moth in the dark against the screen,
and every far sound called the listening out   ·
into places where the rest of us had never been.

More spoke to him from the soft wild night
than came to our porch for us on the wind;
we would watch him look up and his face go keen
till the walls of the world flared, widened.

My father heard so much that we still stand
inviting the quiet by turning the face,
waiting for a time when something in the night
will touch us too from that other place.

Clash

The butcher knife was there
on the table my father made.
The hatchet was on the stair;
I knew where it was.

Hot wires burned in the wall,
all the nails pointed in.
At the sound of my mother's call
I knew it was the time.

When she threatened I hid in the yard.
Policemen would come for me.
It was dark; waiting was hard.
There was something I had to win.

After my mother wept
I forgot where the hatchet was:
there was a truce we kept—
we both chose real things.

If she taunted, I grew still.
If she faltered, I lowered the knife.
I did not have to kill.
Time had made me stronger.

I won before too late,
and—adult before she died—
I had traveled from love to hate,
and partway back again.

Now all I have, my life,
—strange—comes partly from this:
I thought about a knife
when I learned that great word—"Choose."

Our Kind

Our mother knew our worth—
not much. To her, success
was not being noticed at all.
"If we can stay out of jail,"
she said, "God will be proud of us."

"Not worth a row of pins,"
she said, when we looked at the album:
"Grandpa?—ridiculous."
Her hearing was bad, and that
was good: "None of us ever says much."

She sent us forth equipped
for our kind of world, a world of
our betters, in a nation so strong
its greatest claim is no boast,
its leaders telling us all, "Be proud"—

But over their shoulders, God and
our mother, signaling: "Ridiculous."

Aunt Mabel

This town is haunted by some good deed
that reappears like a country cousin, or truth
when language falters these days trying to lie,
because Aunt Mabel, an old lady gone now, would
accost even strangers to give bright flowers
away, quick as a striking snake. It's deeds like this
have weakened me, shaken by intermittent trust,
stricken with friendliness.

Our Senator talked like war, and Aunt Mabel
said, "He's a brilliant man,
but we didn't elect him that much."

Everyone's resolve weakens toward evening
or in a flash when a face melds—a stranger's, even—
reminded for an instant between menace and fear:
There are Aunt Mabels all over the world,
        or their graves in the rain.

At the Grave of My Brother: Bomber Pilot

Tantalized by wind, this flag that flies
to mark your grave discourages those nearby
graves, and all still marching this hillside chanting,
    "Heroes, thanks. Goodby."

If a visitor may quiz a marble sentiment,
was this tombstone quarried in that country
where you slew thousands likewise honored
    of the enemy?

Reluctant hero, drafted again each Fourth
of July, I'll bow and remember you. Who
shall we follow next? Who shall we kill
    next time?

A Catechism

Who challenged my soldier mother?
    Nobody.
Who kept house for her and fended off the world?
    My father.
Who suffered most from her oppressions?
    My sister.
Who went out into the world to right its wrongs?
    My sister.
Who became bitter when the world didn't listen?
    My sister.
Who challenged my soldier sister?
    Nobody.
Who grew up and saw all this and recorded it and
kept wondering how to solve it but couldn't?
    Guess who.

Circle of Breath

The night my father died the moon shone on the snow.
I drove in from the west; mother was at the door.
All the light in the room extended like a shadow.
Truant from knowing, I stood where the great dark fell.

There was a time before, something we used to tell—
how we parked the car in a storm and walked into a field
to know how it was to be cut off, out in the dark alone.
My father and I stood together while the storm went by.

A windmill was there in the field giving its little cry
while we stood calm in ourselves, knowing we could go home.
But I stood on the skull of the world the night he died, and knew
that I leased a place to live with my white breath.

Truant no more, I stepped forward and learned his death.

A Memorial: Son Bret

In the way you went you were important.
I do not know what you found.
In the pattern of my life you stand
where you stood always, in the center,
a hero, a puzzle, a man.

What you might have told me
I will never know—the lips went still,
the body cold. I am afraid
in the circling stars, in the dark,
and even at noon in the light.

When I run what am I running from?
You turned once to tell me something,
but then you glimpsed a shadow on my face
and maybe thought, Why tell what hurts?
You carried it, my boy, so brave, so far.

Now we have all the days, and the sun
goes by the same; there is a faint,
wandering trail I find sometimes, off
through grass and sage. I stop
and listen: only summer again—remember?—

The bees, the wind.

A Family Turn

All her Kamikaze friends admired my aunt,
their leader, charmed in vinegar,
a woman who could blaze with such white blasts
as Lawrence's that lit Arabia.
Her mean opinions bent her hatpins.

We'd take a ride in her old car
that ripped like Sherman through society:
Main Street's oases sheltered no one
when she pulled up at Thirty-first
and whirled that Ford for another charge.

We swept headlines from under rugs, names
all over town, which I learned her way, by heart,
and blazed with love that burns because it's real.
With a turn that's our family's own,
she'd say, "Our town is not the same"—

Pause—"And it's never been."

Ruby Was Her Name

My mother, who opened my eyes, who
brought me into the terrible world,
was guilty. Her look apologized:
she knew what anyone said was true about us
but therefore unfair. How could they blame us
for doing the things we were set to do?

Never heroic, never a model
for us, or for anyone, she cowered
and looked from the corner of her eye—
"Et tu?" And it always meant we were
with her, alas. No one else
could find the center of the world.

She found the truth like a victim; it hit
her again and again, and she always cried out.
At the end she turned to me, helplessly
honest still: "Oh, Bill, I'm afraid,"
and the whole of her life went back to her heart,
from me in a look for the look she gave.

With Kit, Age 7, at the Beach

We would climb the highest dune,
from there to gaze and come down:
the ocean was performing;
we contributed our climb.

Waves leapfrogged and came
straight out of the storm.
What should our gaze mean?
Kit waited for me to decide.

Standing on such a hill,
what would you tell your child?
That was an absolute vista.
Those waves raced far, and cold.

"How far could you swim, Daddy,
in such a storm?"
"As far as was needed," I said,
and as I talked, I swam.

Passing Remark

In scenery I like flat country.
In life I don't like much to happen.

In personalities I like mild colorless people.
And in colors I prefer gray and brown.

My wife, a vivid girl from the mountains,
says, "Then why did you choose me?"

Mildly I lower my brown eyes—
there are so many things admirable people do not understand.

Once in the 40s

We were alone one night on a long
road in Montana. This was in winter, a big
night, far to the stars. We had hitched,
my wife and I, and left our ride at
a crossing to go on. Tired and cold—but
brave—we trudged along. This, we said,
was our life, watched over, allowed to go
where we wanted. We said we'd come back some time
when we got rich. We'd leave the others and find
a night like this, whatever we had to give,
and no matter how far, to be so happy again.

One Home

Mine was a Midwest home—you can keep your world.
Plain black hats rode the thoughts that made our code.
We sang hymns in the house; the roof was near God.

The light bulb that hung in the pantry made a wan light,
but we could read by it the names of preserves—
outside, the buffalo grass, and the wind in the night.

A wildcat sprang at Grandpa on the Fourth of July
when he was cutting plum bushes for fuel,
before Indians pulled the West over the edge of the sky.

To anyone who looked at us we said, "My friend";
liking the cut of a thought, we could say "Hello."
(But plain black hats rode the thoughts that made our code.)

The sun was over our town; it was like a blade.
Kicking cottonwood leaves we ran toward storms.
Wherever we looked the land would hold us up.

Prairie Town

There was a river under First and Main;
the salt mines honeycombed farther down.
A wealth of sun and wind ever so strong
converged on that home town, long gone.

At the north edge there were the sandhills.
I used to stare for hours at prairie dogs,
which had their town, and folded their little paws
to stare beyond their fence where I was.

River rolling in secret, salt mines with care
holding your crystals and stillness, north prairie—
what kind of trip can I make, with what old friend,
ever to find a town so widely rich again?

Pioneers, for whom history was walking through dead grass,
and the main things that happened were miles and the time of day—
you built that town, and I have let it pass.
Little folded paws, judge me: I came away.

Ceremony

On the third finger of my left hand
under the bank of the Ninnescah
a muskrat whirled and bit to the bone.
The mangled hand made the water red.

That was something the ocean would remember:
I saw me in the current flowing through the land,
rolling, touching roots, the world incarnadined,
and the river richer by a kind of marriage.

While in the woods an owl started quavering
with drops like tears I raised my arm.
Under the bank a muskrat was trembling
with meaning my hand would wear forever.

In that river my blood flowed on.

The Farm on the Great Plains

A telephone line goes cold;
birds tread it wherever it goes.
A farm back of a great plain
tugs an end of the line.

I call that farm every year,
ringing it, listening, still;
no one is home at the farm,
the line gives only a hum.

Some year I will ring the line
on a night at last the right one,
and with an eye tapered for braille
from the phone on the wall

I will see the tenant who waits—
the last one left at the place;
through the dark my braille eye
will lovingly touch his face.

"Hello, is Mother at home?"
No one is home today.
"But Father—he should be there."
No one—no one is here.

"But you—are you the one . . . ?"
Then the line will be gone
because both ends will be home:
no space, no birds, no farm.

My self will be the plain,
wise as winter is gray,
pure as cold posts go
pacing toward what I know.

One Evening

On a frozen pond a mile north of Liberal
almost sixty years ago I skated wild circles
while a strange pale sun went down.

A scattering of dry brown reeds cluttered
the ice at one end of the pond, and a fitful
breeze ghosted little surface eddies of snow.

No house was in sight, no tree, only
the arched wide surface of the earth
holding the pond and me under the sky.

I would go home, confront all my years, the tangled
events to come, and never know more than I did
that evening waving my arms in the lemon-colored light.

In the Oregon Country

From old Fort Walla Walla and the Klickitats
to Umpqua near Port Orford, stinking fish tribes
massacred our founders, the thieving whites.

Chief Rotten Belly slew them at a feast;
Kamiakin riled the Snakes and Yakimas;
all spurted arrows through the Cascades west.

Those tribes became debris on their own lands:
Captain Jack's wide face above the rope,
his Modoc women dead with twitching hands.

The last and the most splendid, Nez Percé
Chief Joseph, fluttering eagles through Idaho,
dashed his pony-killing getaway.

They got him. Repeating rifles bored at his head,
and in one fell look Chief Joseph saw the game
out of that spiral mirror all explode.

Back of the Northwest map their country goes,
mountains yielding and hiding fold on fold,
gorged with yew trees that were good for bows.

At the Klamath Berry Festival

The war chief danced the old way—
the eagle wing he held before his mouth—
and when he turned the boom-boom
stopped. He took two steps. A sociologist
was there; the Scout troop danced.
I envied him the places where he had not been.

The boom began again. Outside he heard
the stick game, and the Blackfoot gamblers
arguing at poker under lanterns.
Still-moccasined and bashful, holding
the eagle wing before his mouth,
listening and listening, he danced after others stopped.

He took two steps, the boom caught up,
the mountains rose, the still deep river
slid but never broke its quiet.
I looked back when I left:
he took two steps, he took two steps,
past the sociologist.

Looking for Gold

A flavor like wild honey begins
when you cross the river. On a sandbar
sunlight stretches out its limbs, or is it
a sycamore, so brazen, so clean and bold?
You forget about gold. You stare—and a flavor
is rising all the time from the trees.
Back from the river, over by a thick
forest, you feel the tide of wild honey
flooding your plans, flooding the hours
till they waver forward looking back. They can't
return: that river divides more than
two sides of your life. The only way
is farther, breathing that country, becoming
wise in its flavor, a native of the sun.

An Oregon Message

When we first moved here, pulled
the trees in around us, curled
our backs to the wind, no one
had ever hit the moon—no one.
Now our trees are safer than the stars,
and only other people's neglect
is our precious and abiding shell,
pierced by meteors, radar, and the telephone.

From our snug place we shout
religiously for attention, in order to hide:
only silence or evasion will bring
dangerous notice, the hovering hawk
of the state, or the sudden quiet stare
and fatal estimate of an alerted neighbor.

This message we smuggle out in
its plain cover, to be opened
quietly: Friends everywhere—
we are alive! Those moon rockets
have missed millions of secret
places! Best wishes.

Burn this.

Earth Dweller

It was all the clods at once become
precious; it was the barn, and the shed,
and the windmill, my hands, the crack
Arlie made in the ax handle: oh, let me stay
here humbly, forgotten, to rejoice in it all;
let the sun casually rise and set.
If I have not found the right place,
teach me; for somewhere inside, the clods are
vaulted mansions, lines through the barn sing
for the saints forever, the shed and windmill
rear so glorious the sun shudders like a gong.

Now I know why people worship, carry around
magic emblems, wake up talking dreams
they teach to their children: the world speaks.
The world speaks everything to us.
It is our only friend.

Spirit of Place: Great Blue Heron

Out of their loneliness for each other
two reeds, or maybe two shadows, lurch
forward and become suddenly a life
lifted from dawn or the rain. It is
the wilderness come back again, a lagoon
with our city reflected in its eye.
We live by faith in such presences.

It is a test for us, that thin
but real, undulating figure that promises,
"If you keep faith I will exist
at the edge, where your vision joins
the sunlight and the rain: heads in the light,
feet that go down in the mud where the truth is."

The Fish Counter at Bonneville

Downstream they have killed the river and built a dam;
by that power they wire to here a light:
a turbine strides high poles to spit its flame
at this flume going down. A spot glows white
where an old man looks on at the ghosts of the game
in the flickering twilight—deep dumb shapes that glide.

So many Chinook souls, so many Silverside.

Witness

This is the hand I dipped in the Missouri
above Council Bluffs and found the springs.
All through the days of my life I escort
this hand. Where would the Missouri
meet a kinder friend?

On top of Fort Rock in the sun I spread
these fingers to hold the world in the wind;
along that cliff, in that old cave
where men used to live, I grubbed in the dirt
for those cool springs again.

Summits in the Rockies received this diplomat.
Brush that concealed the lost children yielded
them to this hand. Even on the last morning
when we all tremble and lose, I will reach
carefully, eagerly through that rain, at the end—

Toward whatever is there, with this loyal hand.

Bi-Focal

Sometimes up out of this land
a legend begins to move.
Is it a coming near
of something under love?

Love is of the earth only,
the surface, a map of roads
leading wherever go miles
or little bushes nod.

Not so the legend under,
fixed, inexorable,
deep as the darkest mine
the thick rocks won't tell.

As fire burns the leaf
and out of the green appears
the vein in the center line
and the legend veins under there,

So, the world happens twice—
once what we see it as;
second it legends itself
deep, the way it is.

Across Kansas

My family slept those level miles
but like a bell rung deep till dawn
I drove down an aisle of sound,
nothing real but in the bell,
past the town where I was born.

Once you cross a land like that
you own your face more: what the light
struck told a self; every rock
denied all the rest of the world.
We stopped at Sharon Springs and ate—

My state still dark, my dream too long to tell.

Malheur before Dawn

An owl sound wandered along the road with me.
I didn't hear it—I breathed it into my ears.

Little ones at first, the stars retired, leaving
polished little circles on the sky for awhile.

Then the sun began to shout from below the horizon.
Throngs of birds campaigned, their music a tent of sound.

From across a pond, out of the mist,
one drake made a V and said its name.

Some vast animal of air began to rouse
from the reeds and lean outward.

Frogs discovered their national anthem again.
I didn't know a ditch could hold so much joy.

So magic a time it was that I was both brave and afraid.
Some day like this might save the world.

Starting with Little Things

Love the earth like a mole,
fur-near. Nearsighted,
hold close the clods,
their fine-print headlines.
Pat them with soft hands—

But spades, but pink and loving: they
break rock, nudge giants aside,
affable plow.
Fields are to touch:
each day nuzzle your way.

Tomorrow the world.

Mr. Conscience

The meditative crane
with angular zigzag brain
thinks:

What kind of world am I wading in?

Wait.
Stalk fish:

Where does the me begin?

Step.
Flash the thin thinker,
swish,
to kill.

Wades on.
The answer in his bill.

The Well Rising

The well rising without sound,
the spring on a hillside,
the plowshare brimming through deep ground
everywhere in the field—

The sharp swallows in their swerve
flaring and hesitating
hunting for the final curve
coming closer and closer—

The swallow heart from wing beat to wing beat
counseling decision, decision:
thunderous examples. I place my feet
with care in such a world.

Climbing along the River

Willows never forget how it feels
to be young.

Do you remember where you came from?
Gravel remembers.

Even the upper end of the river
believes in the ocean.

Exactly at midnight
yesterday sighs away.

What I believe is,
all animals have one soul.

Over the land they love
they crisscross forever.

Roll Call

Red Wolf came, and Passenger Pigeon,
the Dodo Bird, all the gone or endangered
came and crowded around in a circle,
the Bison, the Irish Elk, waited
silent, the Great White Bear, fluid and strong,
sliding from the sea, streaming and creeping
in the gathering darkness, nose down,
bowing to earth its tapered head,
where the Black-footed Ferret, paws folded,
stood in the center surveying the multitude
and spoke for us all: "Dearly beloved," it said.

Things I Learned Last Week

Ants, when they meet each other,
usually pass on the right.

Sometimes you can open a sticky
door with your elbow.

A man in Boston has dedicated himself
to telling about injustice.
For three thousand dollars he will
come to your town and tell you about it.

Schopenhauer was a pessimist but
he played the flute.

Yeats, Pound, and Eliot saw art as
growing from other art. They studied that.

If I ever die, I'd like it to be
in the evening. That way, I'll have
all the dark to go with me, and no one
will see how I begin to hobble along.

In The Pentagon one person's job is to
take pins out of towns, hills, and fields,
and then save the pins for later.

Ode to Garlic

Sudden, it comes for you
in the cave of yourself where you know
and are lifted by important events.

Say you are dining and it happens:
soaring like an eagle, you are
pierced by a message from the midst of life:

Memory—what holds the days together—touches
your tongue. It is from deep in the earth
and it reaches out kindly, saying, "Hello, Old Friend."

It makes us alike, all offspring of powerful
forces, part of one great embrace of democracy,
united across every boundary.

You walk out generously, giving it back
in a graceful wave, what you've been given.
Like a child again, you breathe on the world, and it shines.

Reading with Little Sister: A Recollection

The stars have died overhead in their great cold.
Beneath us the sled whispers along. Back there
our mother is gone. They tell us, "If you hold on
the dogs will take you home." And they tell us never
to cry. We'll die too, they say, if we
are ever afraid. All night we hold on.
The stars go down. We are never afraid.

Just Thinking

Got up on a cool morning. Leaned out a window.
No cloud, no wind. Air that flowers held
for awhile. Some dove somewhere.

Been on probation most of my life. And
the rest of my life been condemned. So these moments
count for a lot—peace, you know.

Let the bucket of memory down into the well,
bring it up. Cool, cool minutes. No one
stirring, no plans. Just being there.

This is what the whole thing is about.

Any Morning

Just lying on the couch and being happy.
Only humming a little, the quiet sound in the head.
Trouble is busy elsewhere at the moment, it has
so much to do in the world.

People who might judge are mostly asleep; they can't
monitor you all the time, and sometimes they forget.
When dawn flows over the hedge you can
get up and act busy.

Little corners like this, pieces of Heaven
left lying around, can be picked up and saved.
People won't even see that you have them,
they are so light and easy to hide.

Later in the day you can act like the others.
You can shake your head. You can frown.

First Grade

In the play Amy didn't want to be
anybody; so she managed the curtain.
Sharon wanted to be Amy. But Sam
wouldn't let anybody be anybody else—
he said it was wrong. "All right," Steve said,
"I'll be me, but I don't like it."
So Amy was Amy, and we didn't have the play.
And Sharon cried.

Freedom

Freedom is not following a river.
Freedom is following a river,
    though, if you want to.
It is deciding now by what happens now.
It is knowing that luck makes a difference.

No leader is free; no follower is free—
    the rest of us can often be free.
Most of the world are living by
creeds too odd, chancy, and habit-forming
    to be worth arguing about by reason.

If you are oppressed, wake up about
four in the morning: most places,
you can usually be free some of the time
    if you wake up before other people.

When I Met My Muse

I glanced at her and took my glasses
off—they were still singing. They buzzed
like a locust on the coffee table and then
ceased. Her voice belled forth, and the
sunlight bent. I felt the ceiling arch, and
knew that nails up there took a new grip
on whatever they touched. "I am your own
way of looking at things," she said. "When
you allow me to live with you, every
glance at the world around you will be
a sort of salvation." And I took her hand.

You and Art

Your exact errors make a music
that nobody hears.
Your straying feet find the great dance,
walking alone.
And you live on a world where stumbling
always leads home.

Year after year fits over your face—
when there was youth, your talent
was youth;
later, you find your way by touch
where moss redeems the stone;

And you discover where music begins
before it makes any sound,
far in the mountains where canyons go
still as the always-falling, ever-new flakes of snow.

The Animal That Drank Up Sound

1

One day across the lake where echoes come now
an animal that needed sound came down. He gazed
enormously, and instead of making any, he took
away from, sound: the lake and all the land
went dumb. A fish that jumped went back like a knife,
and the water died. In all the wilderness around he
drained the rustle from the leaves into the mountainside
and folded a quilt over the rocks, getting ready
to store everything the place had known; he buried—
thousands of autumns deep—the noise that used to come there.

Then that animal wandered on and began to drink
the sound out of all the valleys—the croak of toads,
and all the little shiny noise grass blades make.
He drank till winter, and then looked out one night
at the stilled places guaranteed around by frozen
peaks and held in the shallow pools of starlight.
It was finally tall and still, and he stopped on the highest
ridge, just where the cold sky fell away
like a perpetual curve, and from there he walked on silently,
and began to starve.

When the moon drifted over the night the whole world lay
just like the moon, shining back that still
silver, and the moon saw its own animal dead
on the snow, its dark absorbent paws and quiet
muzzle, and thick, velvet, deep fur.

2

After the animal that drank sound died, the world
lay still and cold for months, and the moon yearned
and explored, letting its dead light float down
the west walls of canyons and then climb its delighted
soundless way up the east side. The moon
owned the earth its animal had faithfully explored.
The sun disregarded the life it used to warm.

But on the north side of a mountain, deep in some rocks,
a cricket slept. It had been hiding when that animal
passed, and as spring came again this cricket waited,
afraid to crawl out into the heavy stillness.
Think how deep the cricket felt, lost there
in such a silence—the grass, the leaves, the water,
the stilled animals all depending on such a little
thing. But softly it tried—"Cricket!"—and back like a river
from that one act flowed the kind of world we know,
first whisperings, then moves in the grass and leaves;
the water splashed, and a big night bird screamed.

It all returned, our precious world with its life and sound,
where sometimes loud over the hill the moon,
wild again, looks for its animal to roam, still,
down out of the hills, any time.
But somewhere a cricket waits.

It listens now, and practices at night.

Keeping a Journal

At night it was easy for me with my little candle
to sit late recording what happened that day. Sometimes
rain breathing in from the dark would begin softly
across the roof and then drum wildly for attention.
The candle flame would hunger after each wafting
of air. My pen inscribed thin shadows that leaned
forward and hurried their lines along the wall.

More important than what was recorded, these evenings
deepened my life: they framed every event
or thought and placed it with care by the others.
As time went on, that scribbled wall—even if
it stayed blank—became where everything
recognized itself and passed into meaning.

Indian Caves in the Dry Country

There are some canyons
we might use again
sometime.

Burning a Book

Protecting each other, right in the center
a few pages glow a long time.
The cover goes first, then outer leaves
curling away, then spine and a scattering.
Truth, brittle and faint, burns easily,
its fire as hot as the fire lies make—
flame doesn't care. You can usually find
a few charred words in the ashes.

And some books ought to burn, trying for character
but just faking it. More disturbing
than book ashes are whole libraries that no one
got around to writing—desolate
towns, miles of unthought-in cities,
and the terrorized countryside where wild dogs
own anything that moves. If a book
isn't written, no one needs to burn it—
ignorance can dance in the absence of fire.

So I've burned books. And there are many
I haven't even written, and nobody has.

Growing Up

One of my wings beat faster,
I couldn't help it—
the one away from the light.

It hurt to be told all the time
how I loved that terrible flame.

A Farewell, Age Ten

While its owner looks away I touch the rabbit.
Its long soft ears fold back under my hand.
Miles of yellow wheat bend; their leaves
rustle away and wait for the sun and wind.

This day belongs to my uncle. This is his farm.
We have stopped on our journey; when my father says to
we will go on, leaving this paradise, leaving
the family place. We have my father's job.

Like him, I will be strong all of my life.
We are men. If we squint our eyes in the sun
we will see far. I'm ready. It's good, this resolve.
But I will never pet the rabbit again.

Artist, Come Home

Remember how bright it is,
the old rabbitbush by the hall light?

One of the blackberry vines has
reached all the way to the clothesline.

There isn't any way to keep
the kitchen window from tapping.

The tea kettle had one of its meditative
spells yesterday.

I am thinking again of that old
plan—breakfast first, then the newspaper.

They say maybe they won't have
that big war this year after all.

A frog is living under the
back step.

An Archival Print

God snaps your picture—don't look away—
this room right now, your face tilted
exactly as it is before you can think
or control it. Go ahead, let it betray
all the secret emergencies and still hold
that partial disguise you call your character.

Even your lip, they say, the way it curves
or doesn't, or can't decide, will deliver
bales of evidence. The camera, wide open,
stands ready; the exposure is thirty-five years
or so—after that you have become
whatever the veneer is, all the way through.

Now you want to explain. Your mother
was a certain—how to express it?—*influence.*
Yes. And your father, whatever he was,
you couldn't change that. No. And your town
of course had its limits. Go on, keep talking—
Hold it. Don't move. That's you forever.

Why I Am a Poet

My father's gravestone said, "I knew it was time."
Our house was alive. It moved,
it had a song. The singers back home
all stood in rows along the railroad line.

When the wind came along the track
every neighbor sang. In the last
house I followed the wind—it
left the world and went on.

We knew, the wind and I, that space
ahead of us, the world like an empty room.
I looked back where the sky came down.
Some days no train would come.

Some birds didn't have a song.

Run before Dawn

Most mornings I get away, slip out
the door before light, set forth on the dim, gray
road, letting my feet find a cadence
that softly carries me on. Nobody
is up—all alone my journey begins.

Some days it's escape: the city is burning
behind me, cars have stalled in their tracks,
and everybody is fleeing like me but some other direction.
My stride is for life, a far place.

Other days it is hunting: maybe some game will cross
my path and my stride will follow for hours, matching
all turns. My breathing has caught the right beat
for endurance; familiar trancelike scenes glide by.

And sometimes it's a dream of motion, streetlights coming near,
passing, shadows that lean before me, lengthened
then fading, and a sound from a tree: a soul, or an owl.

These journeys are quiet. They mark my days with adventure
too precious for anyone else to share, little gems
of darkness, the world going by, and my breath, and the road.

The Last Class

They crowd near. If you look at them
they look down. Pause. They shuffle their feet.
Over near the windows along one side
patches of light shine on the floor.
It is almost the hour to begin
whatever comes after this day.

Over their heads you see so many
clouds and stars and days. A hook
begins to come down from the sky.
If you call out, if you warn them,
what good will that do? It is the long
moment that always opens at such times.

Now the eyes turn away. A new
high-pitched hum has compelled the others
to look around. What happens next?
You look toward the exit; this isn't
your place any more. It was coming;
now it is here, the call. Not for them—

For you. It is for you.

Looking across the River

We were driving the river road.
It was at night. "There's the island,"
someone said. And we all looked across
at the light where the hermit lived.

"I'd be afraid to live there"—
it was Ken the driver who spoke.
He shivered and let us feel
the fear that made him shake.

Over to that dark island
my thought had already crossed—
I felt the side of the house
and the night wind unwilling to rest.

For the first time in all my life
I became someone else:
it was dark; others were going their way;
the river and I kept ours.

We came on home that night;
the road led us on. Everything
we said was louder—it was hollow,
and sounded dark like a bridge.

Somewhere I had lost someone—
so dear or so great or so fine
that I never cared again: as if
time dimmed, and color and sound were gone.

Come for me now, World—
whatever is near, come close.
I have been over the water
and lived there all alone.

Father and Son

No sound—a spell—on, on out
where the wind went, our kite sent back
its thrill along the string that
sagged but sang and said, "I'm here!
I'm here!"—till broke somewhere,
gone years ago, but sailed forever clear
of earth. I hold—whatever tugs
the other end—I hold that string.

Choosing a Dog

"It's love," they say. You touch
the right one and a whole half of the universe
wakes up, a new half.

Some people never find
that half, or they neglect it or trade it
for money or success and it dies.

The faces of big dogs tell, over the years,
that size is a burden: you enjoy it for awhile
but then maintenance gets to you.

When I get old I think I'll keep, not a little
dog, but a serious dog,
for the casual, drop-in criminal—

My kind of dog, unimpressed by
dress or manner, just knowing
what's really there by the smell.

Your good dogs, some things that they hear
they don't really want you to know—
it's too grim or ethereal.

And sometimes when they look in the fire
they see time going on and someone alone,
but they don't say anything.

"Are you Mr. William Stafford?"

"Are you Mr. William Stafford?"
"Yes, but. . . ."

Well, it was yesterday.
Sunlight used to follow my hand.
And that's when the strange siren-like sound flooded
over the horizon and rushed through the streets of our town.
That's when sunlight came from behind
a rock and began to follow my hand.

"It's for the best," my mother said—"Nothing can
ever be wrong for anyone truly good."
So later the sun settled back and the sound
faded and was gone. All along the streets every
house waited, white, blue, gray; trees
were still trying to arch as far as they could.

You can't tell when strange things with meaning
will happen. I'm [still] here writing it down
just the way it was. "You don't have to
prove anything," my mother said. "Just be ready
for what God sends." I listened and put my hand
out in the sun again. It was all easy.

Well, it was yesterday. And the sun came,
Why
It came.

Smoke

Smoke's way's a good way—find,
or be rebuffed and gone:
a day and a day, the whole world home.

Smoke? Into the mountains I guess
a long time ago. Once here, yes,
everywhere. Say anything? No.

I saw Smoke, slow traveler, reluctant
but sure. Hesitant sometimes, yes,
because that's the way things are.

Smoke never doubts though:
some new move will appear.
Wherever you are, there is another door.

WILLIAM STAFFORD (1914–1993) was born in Hutchinson, Kansas. In his early years he worked a variety of jobs—in sugar beet fields, in construction, at an oil refinery—and received his bachelor's and master's degrees from the University of Kansas. A conscientious objector and pacifist, he spent the years 1942–1946 in Arkansas and California work camps in the Civilian Public Service, fighting forest fires, building and maintaining trails and roads, halting soil erosion, and beginning his habit of rising early every morning to write. After the war he taught high school, worked for Church World Service, and joined the English faculty of Lewis & Clark College in Portland, Oregon, where he taught until his retirement. He received his PhD from the University of Iowa. He married Dorothy Hope Frantz in 1944, and they were the parents of four children.

Stafford was the author of more than sixty books, the first of which, *West of Your City*, was published when he was forty-six. He received the 1963 National Book Award for *Traveling through the Dark*. He served as Poetry Consultant for the Library of Congress from 1970–1971 and was appointed Oregon State Poet Laureate in 1975. He received the Shelley Award from the Poetry Society of America. An enormously loved and admired writer, a generous mentor to aspiring poets everywhere, Stafford traveled thousands of miles in his later years, giving hundreds of readings in colleges and universities, community centers and libraries, throughout the United States and in Egypt, India, Bangladesh, Pakistan, Iran, Germany, Austria, and Poland. Since his death in 1993, his poetry has been collected in *The Way It Is: New and Selected Poems* and in *Another World Instead: The Early Poems of William Stafford 1937–1947*.

Book design by Rachel Holscher. Composition by BookMobile Design & Digital Publisher Services, Minneapolis, Minnesota. Manufactured by Versa Press on acid-free, 30 percent postconsumer wastepaper.